GRANDPA

A story to help children cope positively with bereavement

In memory of my Grandpa, Stephen Creed.

'Grandpa' Edition published 2020

Original title 'Grandad' first published in Great Britain in 2016 by Books By Sarah Publishing
Text and illustrations copyright © Sarah Hewitt 2016

ISBN 9798636909583

The right of Sarah Hewitt to be identified as the Author and Illustrator of The Work has been asserted by her
in accordance with the Copyright, Design and Patents Act of 1988. All rghts reserved.
No part of this publication may be reproduced, stored in a retrieval system, or transmitted, in any form, or by any means,
electrical, mechanical, photocopying, recording or otherwise without prior permission of the publisher
or a licence permissing restricted copying.

In the United Kingdom such licences are issued by the Copyright Licensing Agency,
Barnard's Inn, 86 Fetter Lane, London EC4A 1EN

GRANDPA

Written and illustrated by Sarah Hewitt

Grandpa is funny and happy with twinkly eyes.
Sarah loves her Grandpa.

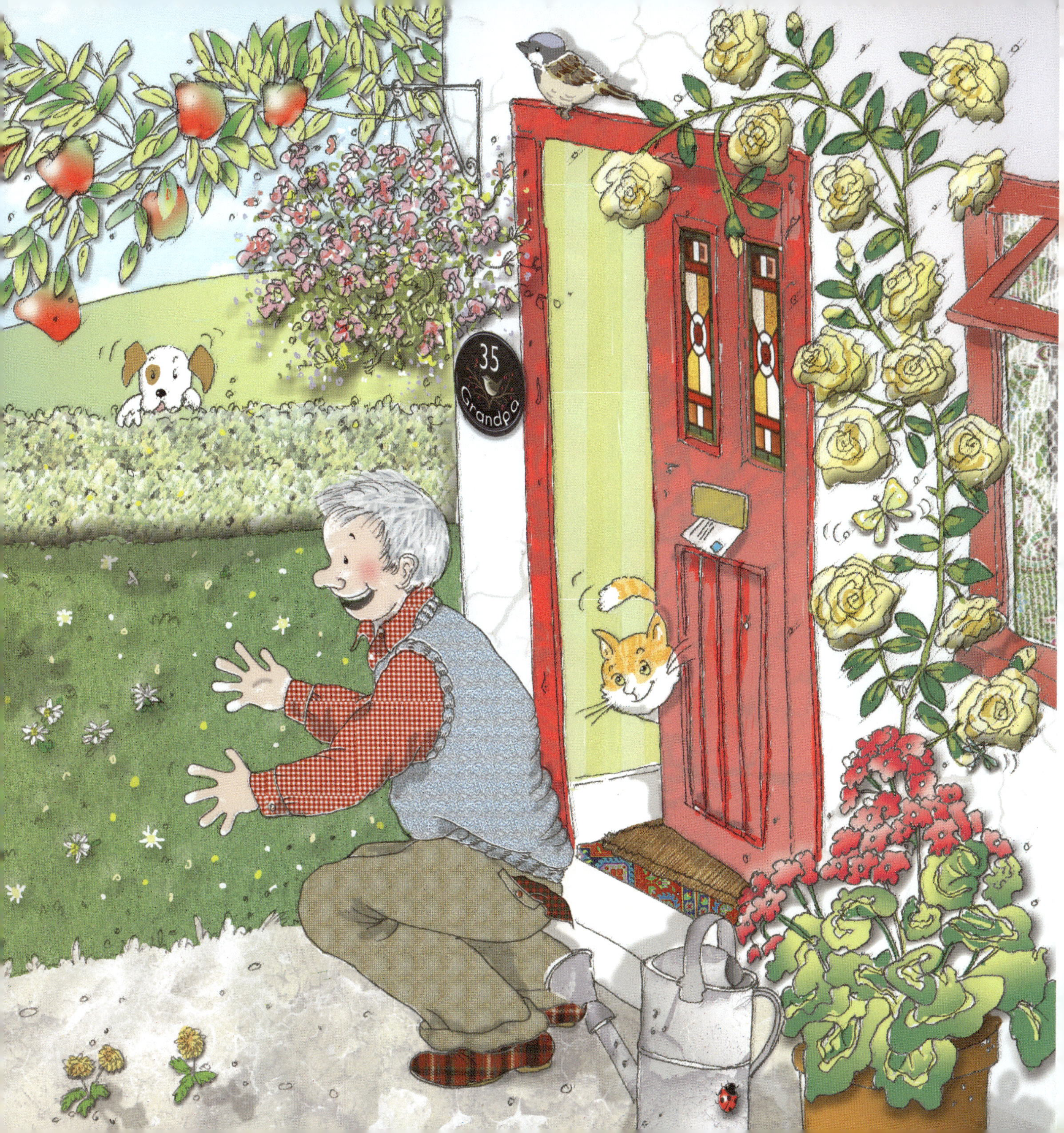
35
Grandpa

Sarah and Grandpa paint colourful pictures together.

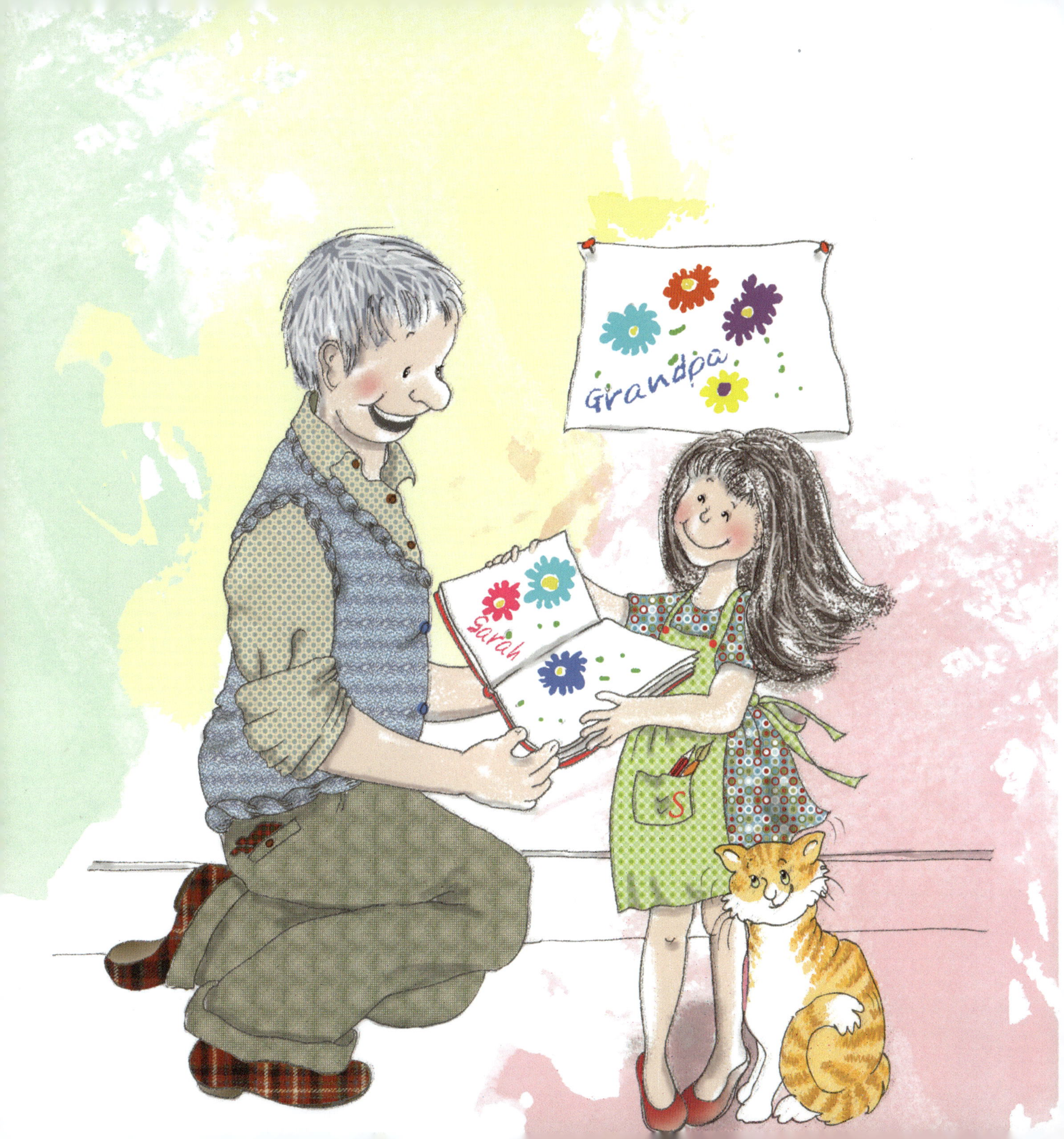
Grandpa
Sarah
S

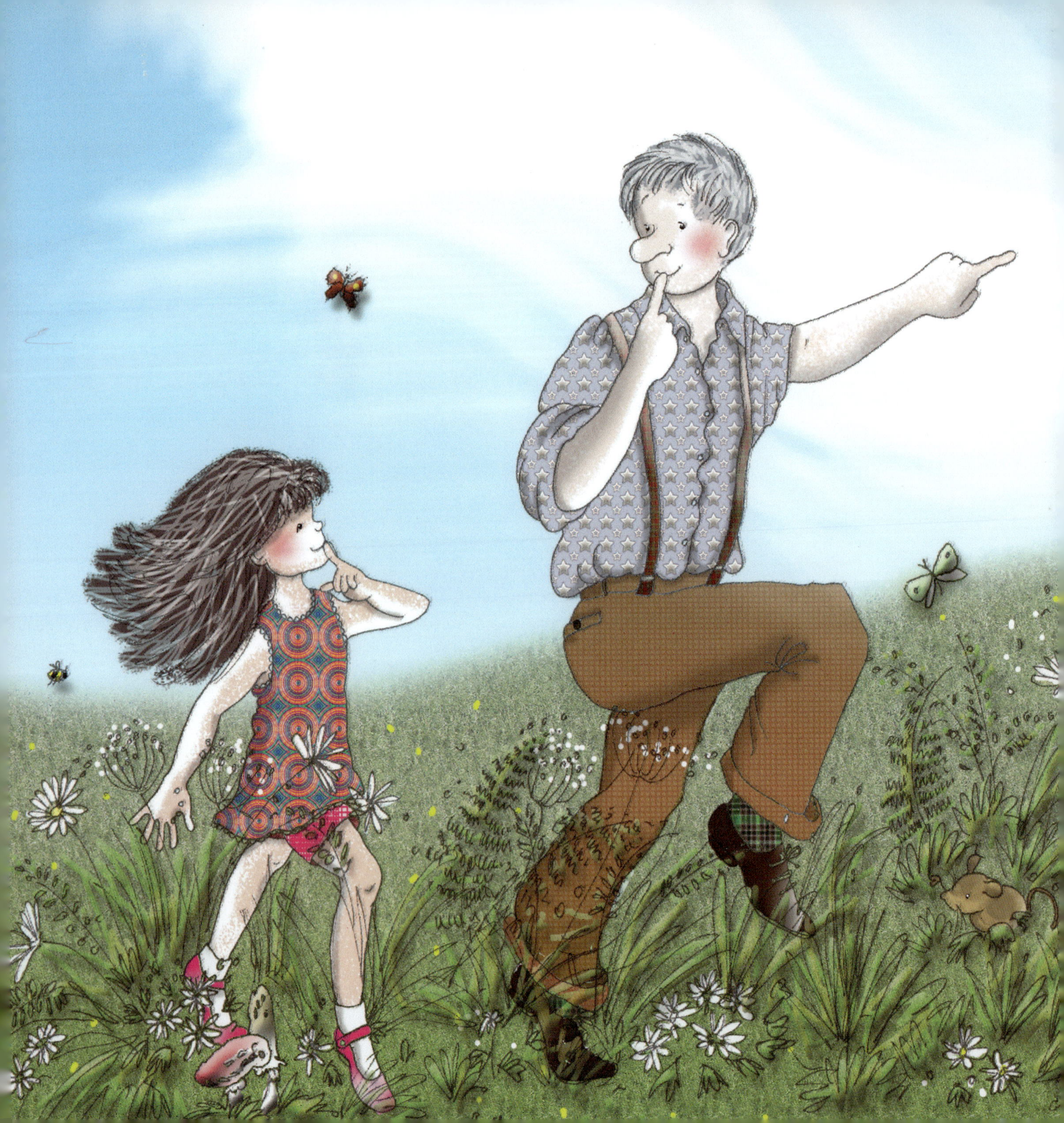

When the sun shines they go on an adventure.
They have to be very quiet so the bears don't hear them.

At bedtime, Grandpa tells magical stories.

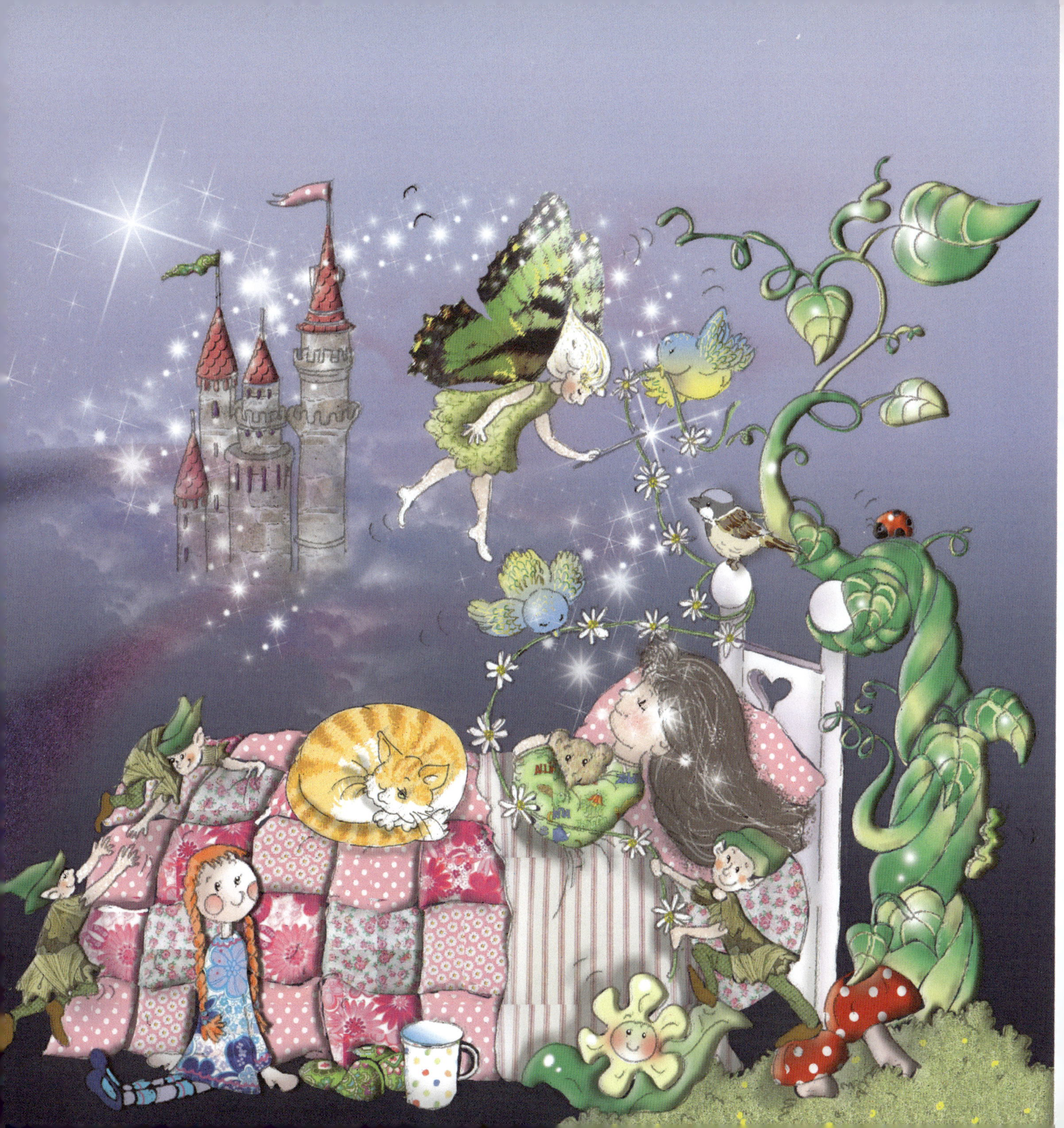

When they wake up, a bird is looking through the window.

Grandpa says the bird is a sparrow.

Later, Grandpa whistles and twirls Sarah round and round. Sparrow sings as they dance.

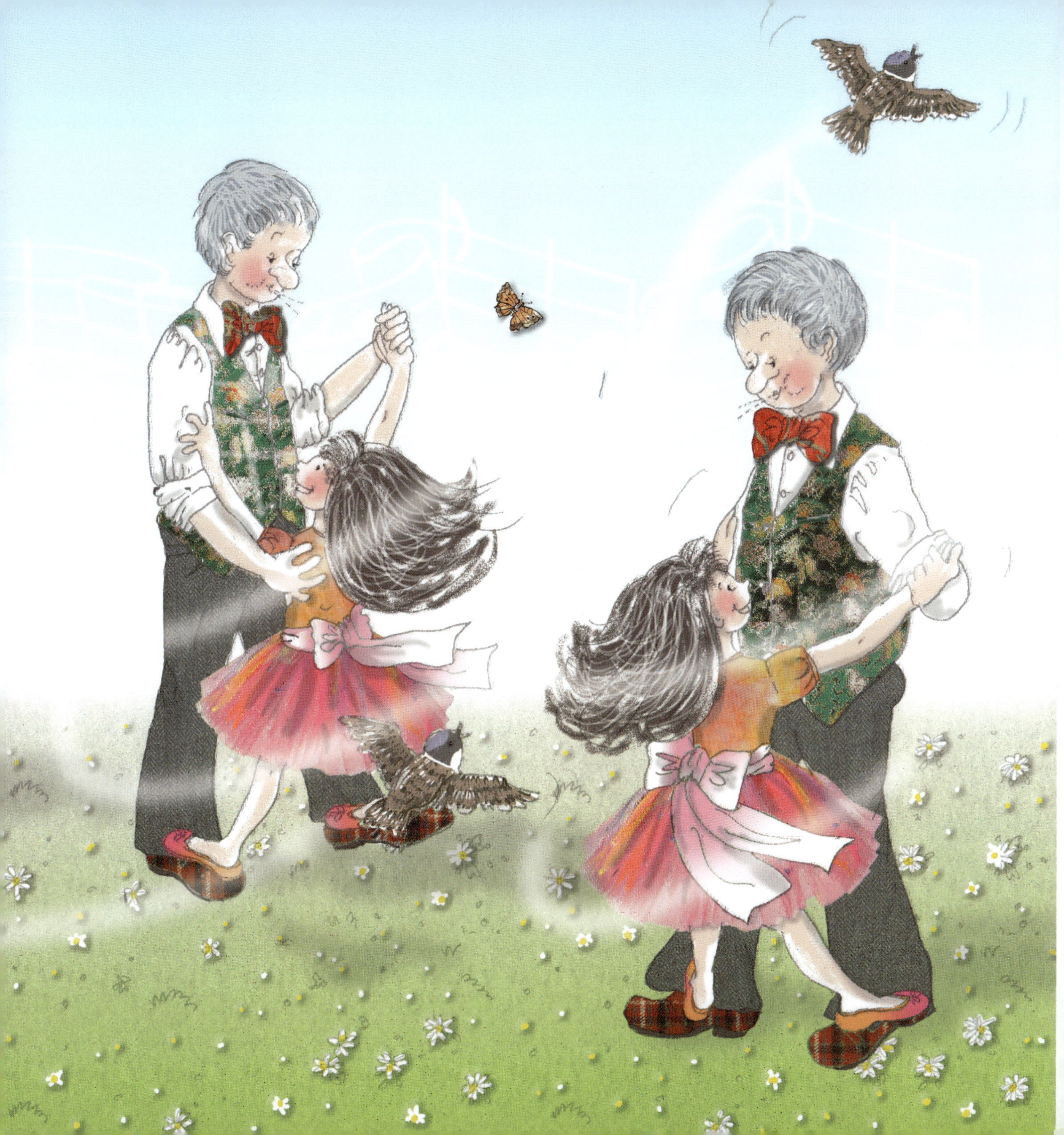

After tea, Sarah sees Sparrow watching them.

Sarah loves Sparrow.

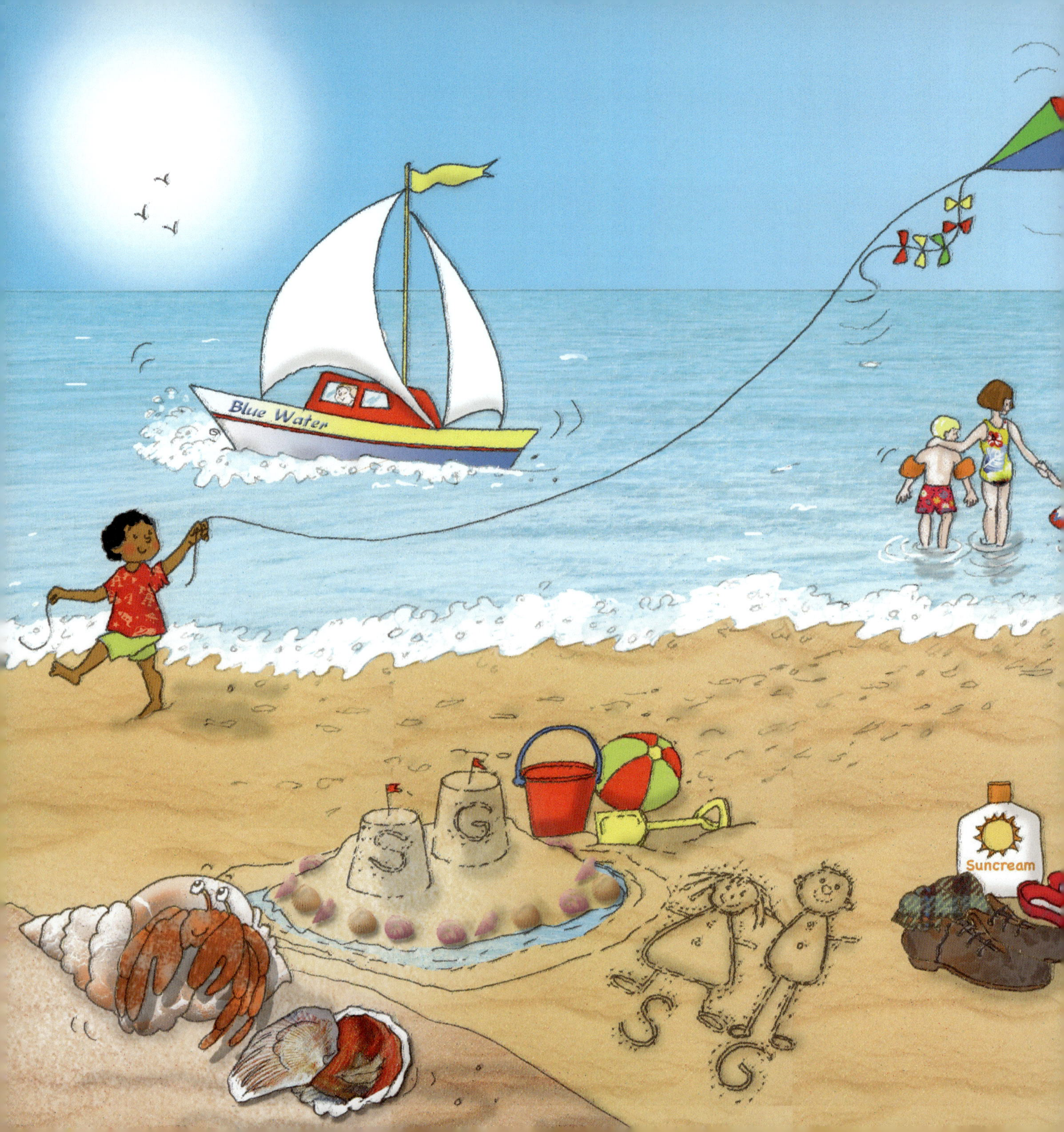
Blue Water
S
G
Suncream
S
G

The next day, Grandpa takes Sarah to the beach.
They have lots of fun!

But when they get home, Sparrow is lying on the grass.

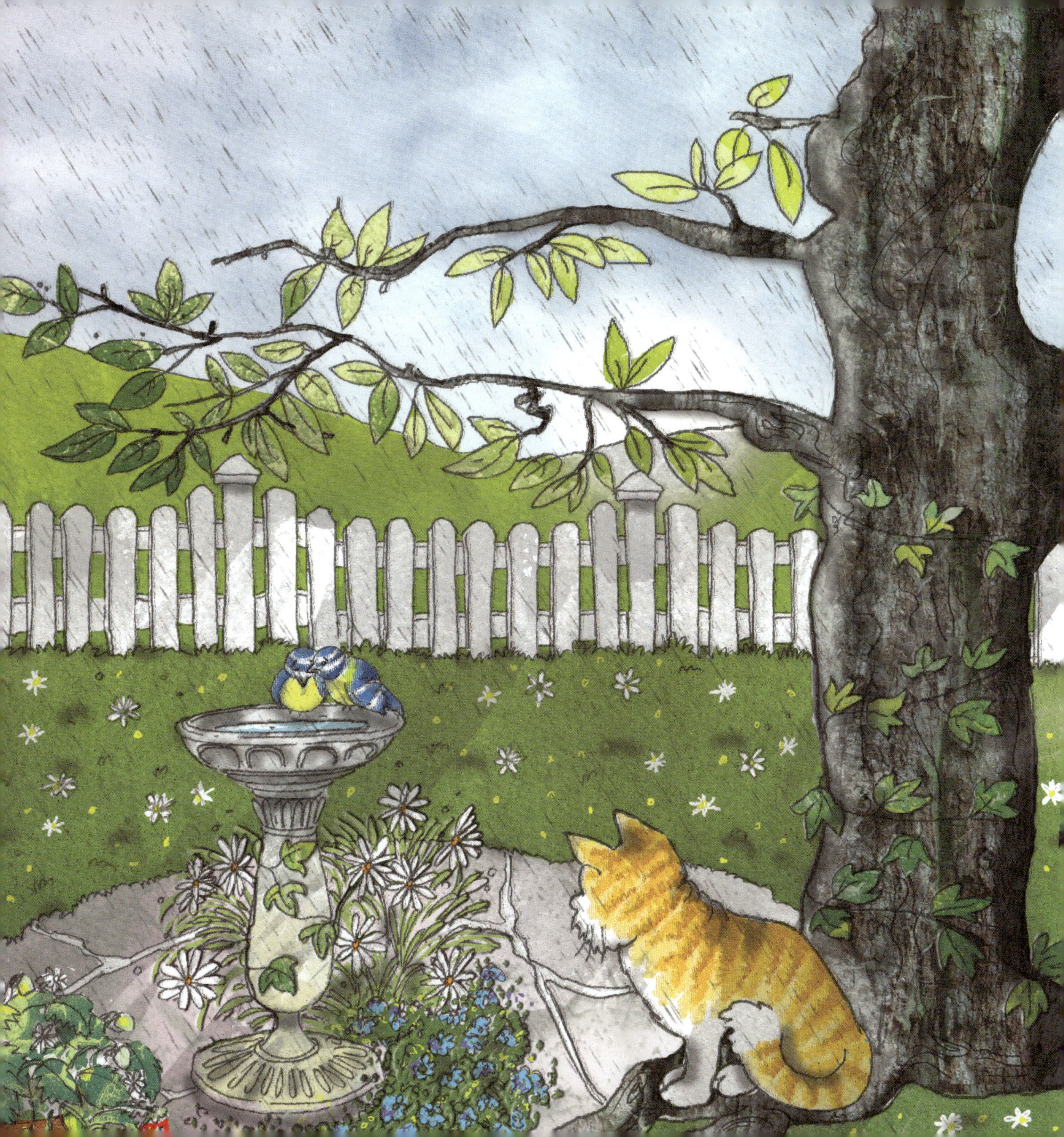

Grandpa says Sparrow has died.
Sarah feels sad.

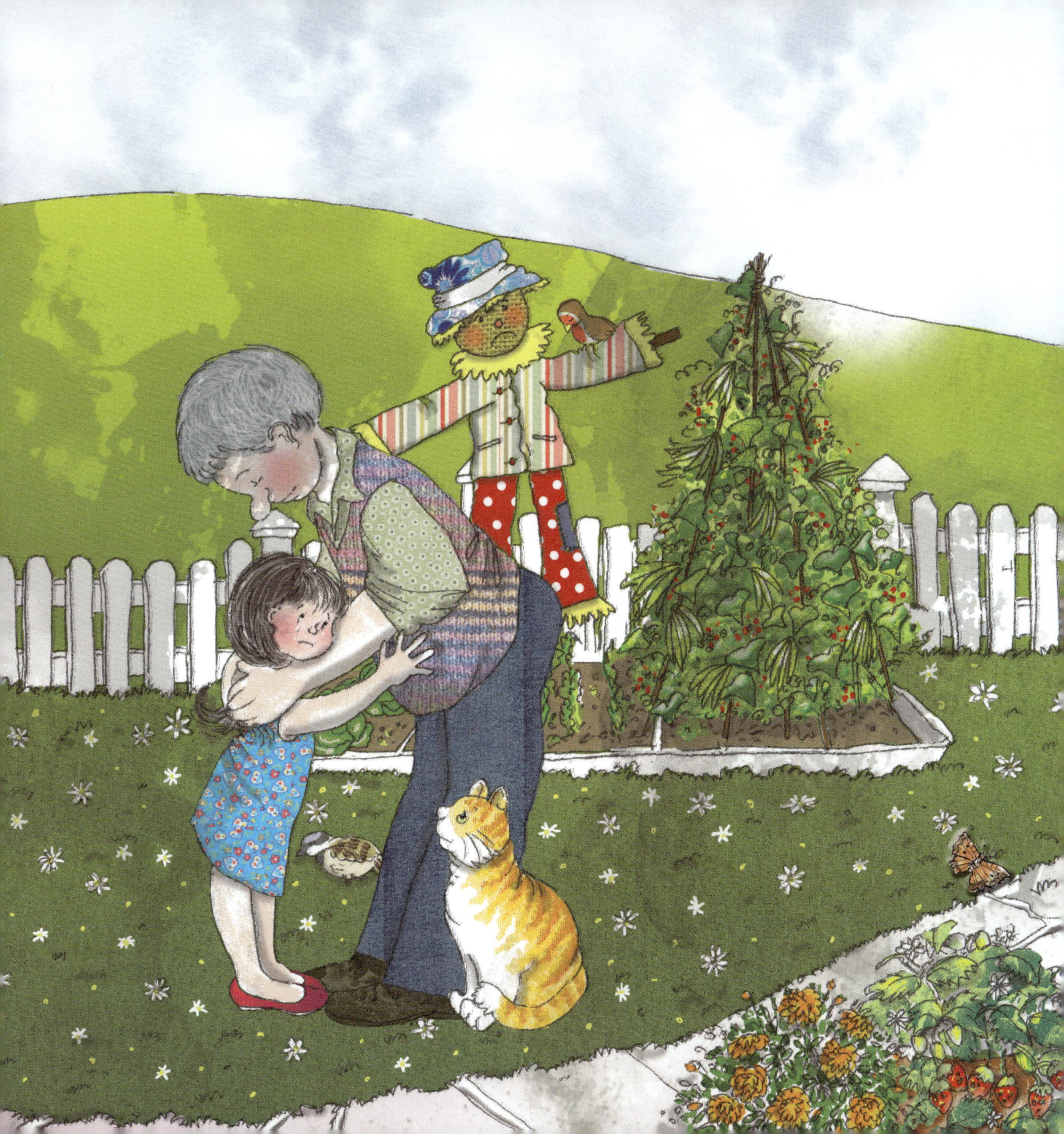

Grandpa says that if we think about who we love they will always be with us.

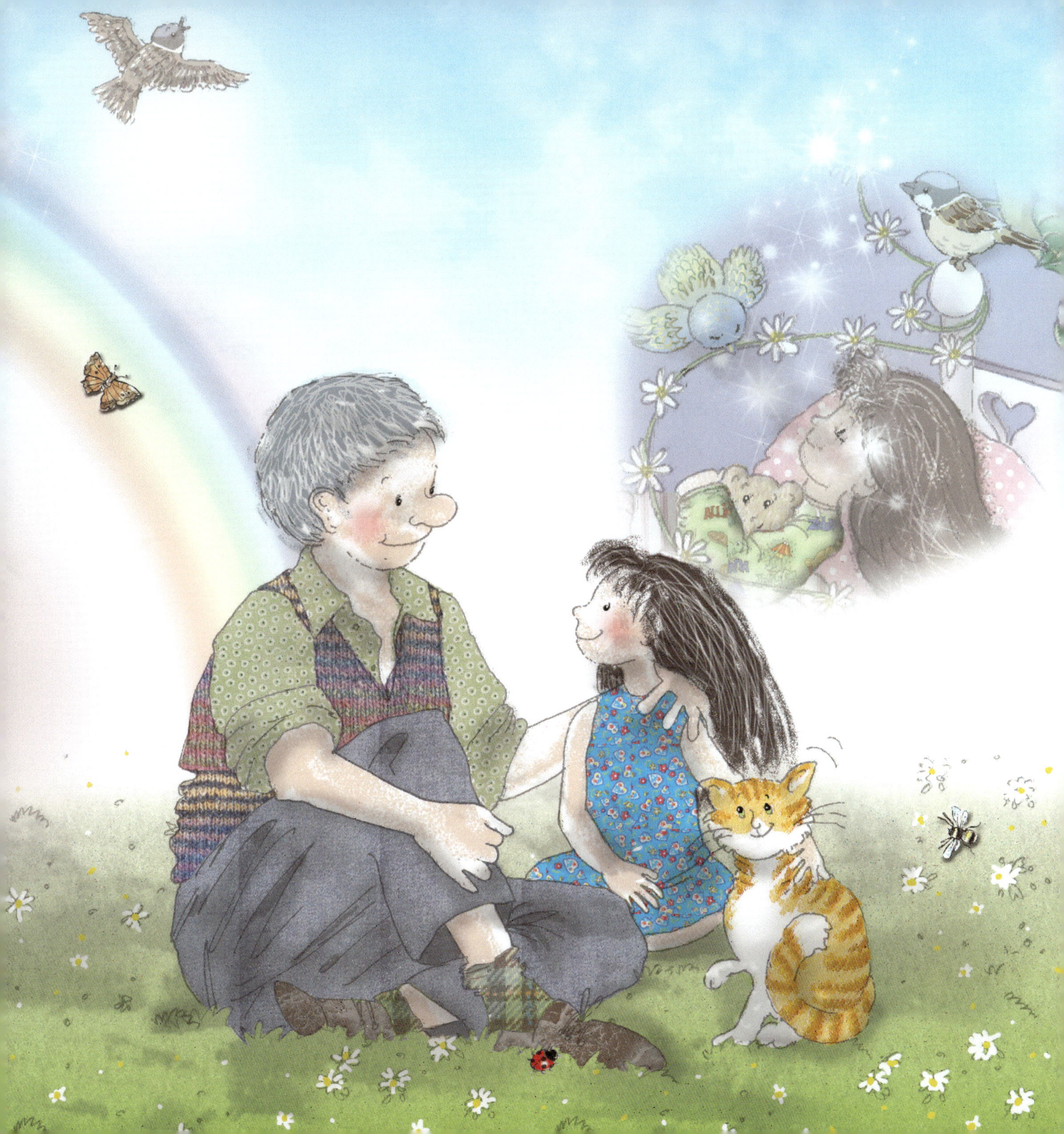

Sarah is grown up now.
She thinks about Grandpa and he is always with her.

Sarah loves her Grandpa.

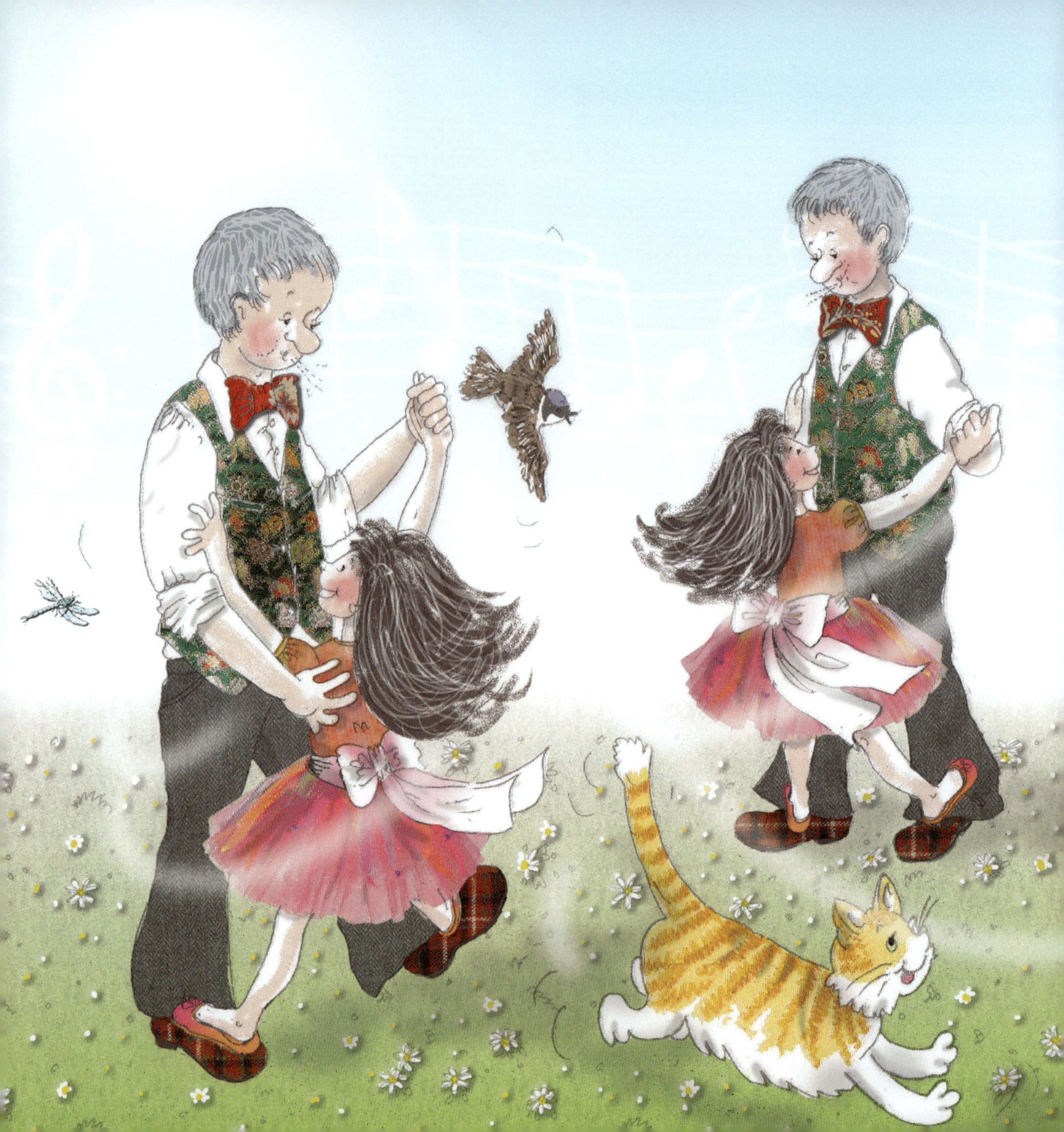

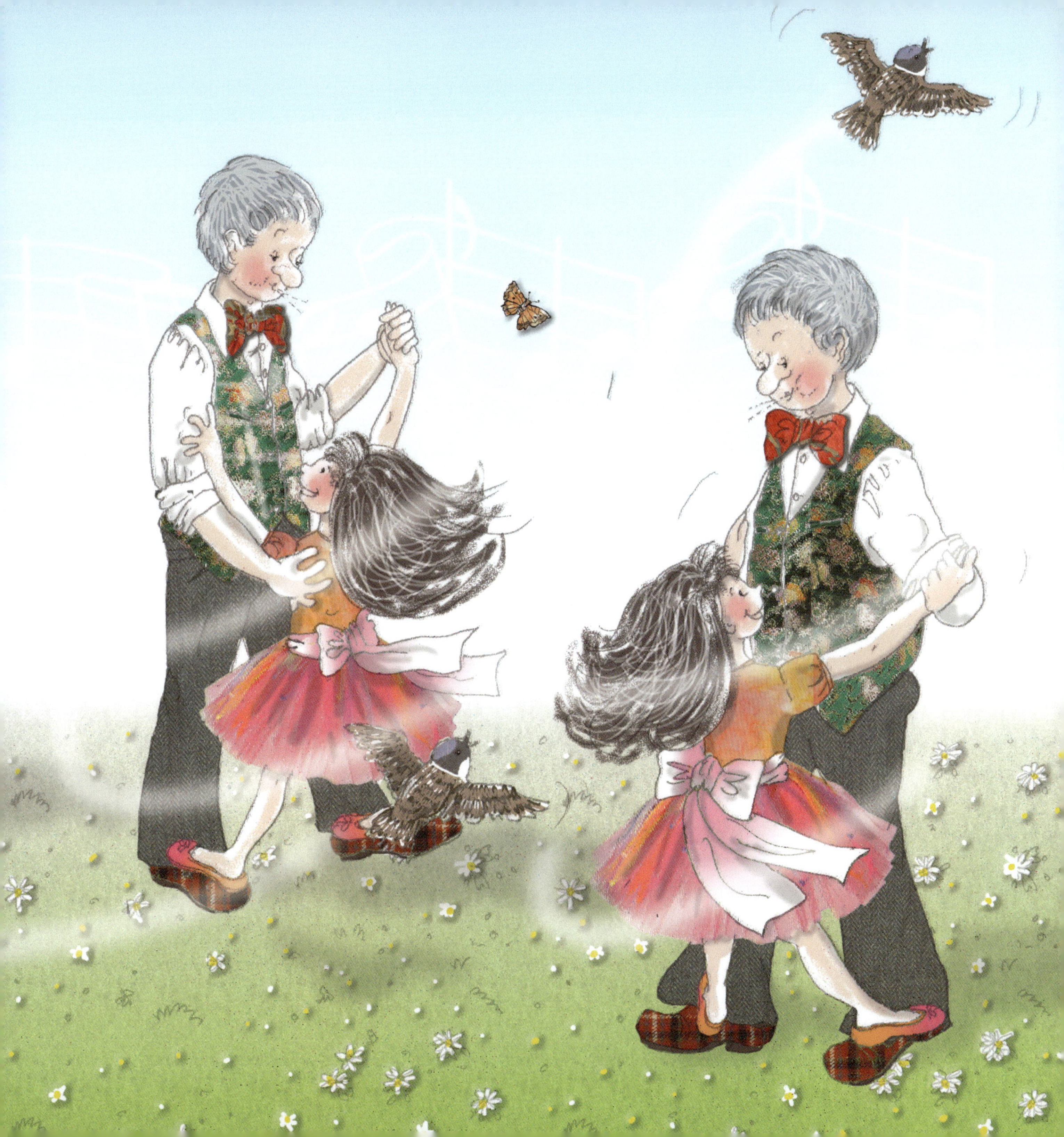

From the author:

Thank you for reading 'Grandpa'

Please leave me a review on Amazon.
To learn about more of my books or to send me a messsage,
please visit my website at www.booksbysarah.co.uk

Printed in Great Britain
by Amazon